THE   INCARNATION

A

Scripture for Meditation: 10

THE INCARNATION

Henry Wansbrough OSB

 St Paul Publications

ST PAUL PUBLICATIONS
SLOUGH   SL3 6BT   ENGLAND

Nihil obstat: Gerard E. Roberts, Censor
Imprimatur: + Charles Grant, Bishop of Northampton
22 October 1973

CONTENTS

BIBLE PASSAGES USED

1. Genesis 3:8-15
   Revelation 12:1-6
2. Hebrews 7:1-3, 15-19,
   26-27; 8:1
   Romans 5:15-19
3. Genesis 49:8-12
   Mark 4:30-32
   Ephesians 1:18-23
4. 2 Samuel 7:4-16
   Mark 9:2-8
5. Psalm 2:7-9
   Hebrews 1:1-5
6. Psalm 110:1-4
   Acts 2:32-36
7. Isaiah 7:10-17
   Matthew 1:18-23
8. Isaiah 9:2-3
   Luke 2:25-32
9. Isaiah 9:6-7
10. Isaiah 11:1-5
11. Isaiah 42:1-4
    Luke 4:16-22
12. Ezekiel 34:11-16, 23
    John 10:7-8, 10-15
13. Malachi 3:1-3
    Matthew 3:7-12
14. Wisdom 7:22-81
    Colossians 1:13-20
15. Deuteronomy 32:39
    John 5:19-21
16. Luke 2:41-52
    Mark 13:32
17. Psalm 107:23-30
    Matthew 14:22-33
18. Isaiah 61:1-3
    Luke 6:20-26
19. Isaiah 52:13 - 53:12
    Matthew 4:1-11
20. Daniel 7:9-14
    Matthew 24:29-31
21. Matthew 25:31-46
    John 5:22-24
22. John 1:1-5, 16-18
    John 14:8-11a
23. John 2:1-11
    John 17:24 - 18:1
24. 1 Corinthians 8:5-6
    1 Corinthians 12:3
25. 1 Thessalonians 5:1-10
    1 Corinthians 16:21-24
    1 Corinthians 15:24-28

ACKNOWLEDGEMENT

The Bible text in this publication is from the Revised Standard Version Bible, Catholic Edition, copyrighted © 1965 and 1966 by the Division of Christian Education of the National Council of the Churches of Christ in the U.S.A., and used by permission.

FOREWORD

In meditating on the Incarnation one is meditating on the central point of all scripture, to which the Old Testament leads up and in which the New Testament blossoms. This is the central point of God's plan for man. That God should confine himself by becoming man is an absurdity, an impossibility which one would not believe, had it not occurred. In this series of meditations we circle round different aspects of this fundamental mystery, seeking to learn and understand with intellect and affection more about God our Father, who is revealed to us in his Son and our Lord, Jesus, and about the dignity of our destiny in Christ.

HENRY WANSBROUGH

Ampleforth
September 1973

7

1

THE SEED OF WOMAN

Genesis 3 : 8-15   *The serpent's head*

And they heard the sound of the Lord God walking in
the garden in the cool of the day, and the man and his
wife hid themselves from the presence of the Lord God
among the trees of the garden. But the Lord God called
to the man, and said to him, "Where are you?" And
he said, "I heard the sound of thee in the garden, and
I was afraid, because I was naked; and I hid myself."
He said, "Who told you that you were naked? Have you
eaten of the tree of which I commanded you not to
eat?" The man said, "The woman whom thou gavest
to be with me, she gave me fruit of the tree, and I ate."
Then the Lord God said to the woman, "What is this
that you have done?" The woman said, "The serpent
beguiled me, and I ate." The Lord God said to the
serpent,
"Because you have done this,
　　cursed are you above all cattle,
　　and above all wild animals;
upon your belly you shall go,
　　and dust you shall eat
　　all the days of your life.
I will put enmity between you and the woman,
　　and between your seed and her seed;
he shall bruise your head,
　　and you shall bruise his heel."

9

Revelation 12 : 1-6   *The great sign in heaven*

And a great portent appeared in heaven, a woman clothed with the sun, with the moon under her feet, and on her head a crown of twelve stars; she was with child and she cried out in her pangs of birth, in anguish for delivery. And another portent appeared in heaven; behold, a great red dragon, with seven heads and ten horns, and seven diadems upon his heads. His tail swept down a third of the stars of heaven, and cast them to the earth. And the dragon stood before the woman who was about to bear a child, that he might devour her child when she brought it forth; she brought forth a male child, one who is to rule all the nations with a rod of iron, but her child was caught up to God and to his throne, and the woman fled into the wilderness, where she has a place prepared by God, in which to be nourished for one thousand two hundred and sixty days.

Reflection

Spanning the diverse collection of writings which make up the holy scriptures are these mentions of a woman and her seed. Both are mysterious, and both have the rich meaning of myth which will not be tied down to a single limiting sense.

The story of the Fall at the beginning of Genesis is couched in historical language, and appears to narrate what once happened in the distant past, at the dawn of humanity. But we shall hit the mark far more closely if we consider it as a reflection upon the state of humanity as it is. The story expresses an awareness that all is not as it should be, that man is far lower and less perfect than God, his creator, intends him to be. This is put in the mythical form of a departure from a state that once was — just as other cultures express this same idea by the myth of a golden age long ago, from which man has gradually declined, until he reaches his present state. In each case the essential is that an ideal exists which is not now being attained. But in Genesis the curse of God on the serpent gives a hope which is unique. The creature which ends up as an odious reptile was, before it was condemned to go on its belly, a much more imposing dragon, representing the pomp and attractiveness of the power of evil. But the hope of mankind is that the seed of woman will scotch the snake. There are no details — details would be out of place in this mythical representation — but only the promise that eventually mankind will triumph, not without cost to himself, over the power of evil; he will not always be in the present unsatisfactory state of grovelling to evil. It is only afterwards, in the light of the victory won by Christ, that we can see that the promise fits his victory perfectly and that the seed of woman in general may be understood of him in particular.

At the other end of the Bible the book of Revelation also promises deliverance from the ravages of the power of evil. Again there is the raging dragon and the woman who is the mother of a man. Does she represent Mary directly and the son Christ, or is she the Church? Perhaps there is no need to decide, for at any rate Mary, in being mother of Christ, is mother of the Church. The Church is Christ's body and triumphs with him over the evil power which oppresses us. A symbolic picture of this kind cannot be tied down to more detail.

Prayer

It is your becoming man, Lord, which has given us the strength to overcome the weight of evil which lies so heavy on us. Enable us to feel the power which you have given us by becoming one of us, and to join you actively in your victory.

2

PRIEST OF THE ORDER OF MELCHIZEDEK

Hebrews 7:1-3, 15-19, 26-27; 8:1 *Christ as Priest*

For this Melchizedek, king of Salem, priest of the Most High God, met Abraham returning from the slaughter of the kings and blessed him; and to him Abraham apportioned a tenth part of everything. He is first, by translation of his name, king of righteousness, and then he is also king of Salem, that is, king of peace. He is without father or mother or genealogy, and has neither beginning of days nor end of life, but resembling the Son of God he continues a priest for ever.

This becomes even more evident when another priest arises in the likeness of Melchizedek, who has become a priest, not according to a legal requirement concerning bodily descent but by the power of an indestructible life. For it is witnessed of him,

"Thou art a priest for ever,
after the order of Melchizedek."

On the one hand, a former commandment is set aside because of its weakness and uselessness (for the law made nothing perfect); on the other hand, a better hope is introduced, through which we draw near to God.

For it was fitting that we should have such a high priest, holy, blameless, unstained, separated from sinners, exalted above the heavens. He has no need, like those high priests, to offer sacrifices daily, first for his own sins and then for those of the people; he did this once for all when he offered up himself.

Now the point in what we are saying is this: we have such a high priest, one who is seated at the right hand of the throne of the Majesty in heaven.

Romans 5:15-19 *The Obedience of Christ*

But the free gift is not like the trespass. For if many died through one man's trespass, much more have the grace of God and the free gift in the grace of that one man Jesus Christ abounded for many. And the free gift is not like the effect of that one man's sin. For the judgment following one trespass brought condemnation, but the free gift following many trespasses brings justification. If, because of one man's trespass, death reigned through that one man, much more will those who receive the abundance of grace and the free gift of righteousness reign in life through the one man Jesus Christ.

Then as one man's trespass led to condemnation for all men, so one man's act of righteousness leads to acquittal and life for all men. For as by one man's disobedience many were made sinners, so by one man's obedience many will be made righteous.

Reflection

Melchizedek is a symbol for the author of Hebrews because as a priest he appears for a fleeting instant from nowhere, and because even God's chosen founder of the holy people recognizes his priesthood and superiority by paying tithes. The author's whole theme is the superiority of Christ's priesthood to that of the Old Law.

The aspect of priesthood is a cardinal one for the incarnation. It is the binding together of what is separate that is important, and Christ by his very nature unites man to God, restoring the harmony that was intended. It is also of the essence of a priest that he acts for others, and again the incarnation makes sense only because Christ acts for others.

Sin is always a prominent idea when we think of sacrifice, and in the present state this is natural because we are so conscious of our sin. This is the aspect which Paul considers in Romans: Christ's obedience undoes man's disobedience; his perfect subjection to God's will, his perfect union to the purpose of the Father, heals the wound made by man's stubborn attempts at independence. But sin touches only one aspect of sacrifice and priesthood, the negative aspect of removal of barriers. There is also the more joyful and positive aspect which concerns the uniting of man to God, which was the purpose of creation.

If one looks at creation from an evolutionary, Teilhardian point of view, the incarnation is the climax towards which creation had been moving by gradual stages of improvement, until it was ready for the intervention of God which was the divinisation of man. In this way God becoming man — or rather man receiving God's nature — is the high-point which was intended by God in any case, even without sin. We need not be ashamed of the incarnation, for it was not only our faults which brought Christ down to patch things up. The incarnation would have made sense even without sin, as the joyful completion of the whole movement of God's creation, when its purpose was brought to fulfilment. As St Leo said, the incarnation brings us really to see not only our sinfulness but our own dignity, in that human nature is raised to God.

Prayer

Father, your Son as leader of humanity has raised our nature so that we may share your life. Grant that through his obedience we may be freed from our sins and enjoy full happiness with you.

3

UNIVERSAL DOMINION

Genesis 49:8-12   *The promise to Judah*

Judah, your brothers shall praise you;
    your hand shall be on the neck of your enemies;
    your father's sons shall bow down before you.
Judah is a lion's whelp;
    from the prey, my son, you have gone up.
He stooped down, he couched as a lion
    and as a lioness; who dares rouse him up?
The sceptre shall not depart from Judah,
    nor the ruler's staff from between his feet,
until he comes to whom it belongs;
    and to him shall be the obedience of the peoples.
Binding his foal to the vine
    and his ass's colt to the choice vine,
he washes his garments in wine
    and his vesture in the blood of grapes;
his eyes shall be red with wine,
    and his teeth white with milk.

Mark 4:30-32   *The mustard seed*

And he said, "With what can we compare the kingdom
of God, or what parable shall we use for it? It is like a
grain of mustard seed, which, when sown upon the
ground, is the smallest of all the seeds on earth; yet
when it is sown it grows up and becomes the greatest

B

of all shrubs, and puts forth large branches, so that the birds of the air can make nests in its shade."

Ephesians 1:18-23   *All things under his feet*

. . . Having the eyes of your hearts enlightened, that you may know what is the hope to which he has called you, what are the riches of his glorious inheritance in the saints, and what is the immeasurable greatness of his power in us who believe, according to the working of his great might which he accomplished in Christ when he raised him from the dead and made him sit at his right hand in the heavenly places, far above all rule and authority and power and dominion, and above every name that is named, not only in this age but also in that which is to come; and he has put all things under his feet and has made him the head over all things for the Church, which is his body, the fullness of him who fills all in all.

Reflection

This promise to the tribe of Judah is one of the blessings supposedly given by Jacob on his children as he comes near to death. As it concerns the distant future it is again open-ended and mysterious, full more of presage than of exact detail. The passage was perhaps written when David, who was sprung from the tribe of Judah, was already on the throne; but its terms are not wholly used up by his rather limited dominion. At the time of Christ it was interpreted of a messiah, the basis of the hope, widespread at the time, that a Jewish ruler would arise to hold sway over the whole world.

The passage from Ephesians shows the fulfilment of this promise: the risen Christ rules not only over the nations but over the whole universe. But what sort of rule is this? Jesus spent much of his time correcting the ideas of the disciples about worldly rule. His kingdom, or king*ship*, is not of this world but is a hidden rule. The parables of the mustard seed and of the seed growing secretly teach that the kingdom has inner power rather than outward pomp. The disciples found this lesson so hard to grasp that even at the moment of the Ascension they were expecting the restoration of political power to Israel. Even today we have difficulty grasping the idea that Christ's rule is really not of this world. The usual criteria just do not apply: seeming success, recognized by men, is irrelevant, status accorded to the Church by secular powers, what men think of the Church or of Christians, even numerical growth, let alone material prosperity and power — all these criteria of success which we automatically use are misleading in the case of Christ's rule. Its real uniqueness lies in that it is a kingship which must be accepted by each individual. It is not a thing which is just present whether one likes it or not, a fact of life like the climate. A person must take it upon himself, welcome it to be a dominant factor in his own behaviour and structure. It is more or less intense and complete according to the degree in which one wishes Christ's rule to be part of one's life. And it is really the rule of God which Christ brought to fulfilment, not his own kingdom, and in this sense it is the completion of creation, the fulfilment of the creator's design.

Prayer

Your Son, O God, was to rule over the nations with a rule which is in our hearts. Help us to accept your offer and to draw your kingdom to ourselves till you are our king and we wholly your subjects.

4

THE SON

2 Samuel 7:4-16 *A promise to David*

But that same night the word of the Lord came to
Nathan, "Go and tell my servant David, 'Thus says the
Lord: Would you build me a house to dwell in? I have
not dwelt in a house since the day I brought up the
people of Israel from Egypt to this day, but I have been
moving about in a tent for my dwelling. In all places
where I have moved with all the people of Israel, did I
speak a word with any of the judges of Israel, whom I
commanded to shepherd my people Israel, saying, "Why
have you not built me a house of cedar?" Now therefore thus you shall say to my servant David, 'Thus says
the Lord of hosts, I took you from the pasture, from
following the sheep, that you should be prince over
my people Israel; and I have been with you wherever
you went, and have cut off all your enemies from before
you; and I will make for you a great name, like the name
of the great ones of the earth. And I will appoint a
place for my people Israel, and will plant them, that
they may dwell in their own place, and be disturbed no
more; and violent men shall afflict them no more, as
formerly, from the time that I appointed judges over
my people Israel; and I will give you rest from all your
enemies. Moreover the Lord declares to you that the
Lord will make you a house. When your days are fulfilled and you lie down with your fathers, I will raise up

your offspring after you, who shall come forth from your body, and I will establish his kingdom. He shall build a house for my name, and I will establish the throne of his kingdom for ever. I will be his father, and he shall be my son. When he commits iniquity, I will chasten him with the rod of men, with the stripes of the sons of men; but I will not take my steadfast love from him, as I took it from Saul, whom I put away from before you. And your house and your kingdom shall be made sure for ever before me; your throne shall be established for ever.' "

Mark 9: 2-8   *The transfiguration*

And after six days Jesus took with him Peter and James and John, and led them up a high mountain apart by themselves; and he was transfigured before them, and his garments became glistening, intensely white, as no fuller on earth could bleach them. And there appeared to them Elijah with Moses; and they were talking to Jesus. And Peter said to Jesus, "Master, it is well that we are here; let us make three booths, one for you and one for Moses and one for Elijah." For he did not know what to say, for they were exceedingly afraid. And a cloud overshadowed them, and a voice came out of the cloud, "This is my beloved Son; listen to him." And suddenly looking around they no longer saw any one with them but Jesus only.

Reflection

To David the Lord promises to give an heir of his house whose sovereignty will last for ever, and to whom the Lord himself will be a father. This promise formed the backbone of all the subsequent history of the Jews, giving them confidence in their future and a sense of direction. The story of the transfiguration shows how this was fulfilled, for the son is there 'guaranteed', as it were, by the voice from heaven. The presence of Moses and Elijah to support him must also mean that he is the completion of the movement in which they played their prominent parts, the fulfilment of the historical purpose of Israel and of God's revelation in the Law and the Prophets.

Yet what do we mean when we call Jesus 'Son of God'? He is no physical son because God is no physical father; there can be no begetting in God. In the Old Testament several figures were called son of God, even the non-Jewish Cyrus, because of the important part they played in the history of Israel (Cyrus was responsible for the return from the Babylonian captivity, when he captured Babylon and sent home all the exiles), and Israel itself is called God's son with all the warmth of affection. So it denotes a very special link with God, a union of will and purpose, a special care and surveillance on the part of God and a special response from the side of man.

This is certainly not all that is meant by the Christian now when he calls Christ son of God. The second Person of the Trinity has a far more complete and total link to the first Person than this. But it does perhaps help towards an understanding of the mystery of the incarnation: Jesus had a real human personality, with a real human mind. He thought like a man, and as a man could not, any more than any other man, contain the thoughts of God. Like other men, he learnt, and he learnt to know himself. One of the most fascinating mysteries of Jesus' personality is how he came to the realisation — as we learn who we are, in the gradual awakening of self-consciousness — that he was God. All this is a consequence of the reality of the incarnation: God became truly and fully man: the human Jesus was son of God.

Prayer

Lord, you are so beyond our ken that we can only dimly conceive you. Yet you became man and took on the limitations and frustrations of our frailty. Your love for us, chosen out of all creation and out of all possible creations, could find no other expression.

5

THE FULLNESS OF REVELATION

Psalm 2:7-9 *"You are my Son"*

I will tell of the decree of the Lord:
He said to me, "You are my son,
    today I have begotten you.

Ask of me, and I will make the nations your heritage,
    and the ends of the earth your possession.

You shall break them with a rod of iron,
    and dash them in pieces like a potter's vessel."

Hebrews 1:1-5 *"Today I have become your father"*

In many and various ways God spoke of old to our
fathers by the prophets; but in these last days he has
spoken to us by a Son, whom he appointed the heir of
all things, through whom also he created the world.
He reflects the glory of God and bears the very stamp
of his nature, upholding the universe by his word of
power. When he had made purification for sins, he
sat down at the right hand of the Majesty on high,
having become as much superior to angels as the name
he has obtained is more excellent than theirs.

For to what angel did God ever say,
"Thou art my Son,
    today I have begotten thee"?

Or again,
    "I will be to him a father,
    and he shall be to me a son"?

Reflection

This psalm is probably a coronation hymn, celebrating
the crowning of a new king, who by his enthronement
has also become son of God. The idea comes into Israel
from Egypt, where the Pharaoh, as being under God's
closest protection and his special representative, was
somehow identified with God. The Israelite tradition
took up this idea and applied it in a modified form to
their own king, expressing the closeness as the relationship of a son. It is one of the richnesses of the Hebrew
tradition that it grew in a fertile soil, and felt itself
able to learn from its neighbours. The stream of revelation is not a direct quasi-telephonic communication from
God to the mind of man, but he used all kinds of events,
circumstances and contacts too show himself to man —
just as nowadays we may learn his will by reflecting
on the events around us. In this way the experience of
God which neighbouring peoples underwent could lead
Israel to knowledge of God. There is no need to think
of the Chosen People as a narrowly insular column,
happily insulated from the stream of history and from
benighted neighbours. God's light has shone in different
ways on many different peoples, all of whom have
brought their own particular truth to add to the richness
of revelation.

Whatever partial revelation there was, however, God
spoke the totality of his Word in the Son. The point of
this, surely, was that the glory of God should become
visible, since Christ bears the stamp of his nature. The
particular point on which Hebrews insist seems to be

the creative power of God made visible in Christ. It is not too easy to see this in the earthly life of Jesus. How the love of God is made visible in Jesus is clear enough in his unlimited patience, sympathy and self-sacrifice. But his creative power is less easy to see unless it be in his command over nature in the miracles, when he calms the storm or walks on the water — in Old Testament poetry ways of expressing the absolute power of God over his creation. By contrast, then, it must be the absolute power of the risen Christ that the author means, for the early Christians were very aware of this, the sovereign rule of Christ over his creation. His power was very much a reality in their lives, bringing the power and guidance of God to be a real force, present and active.

Prayer

The whole of creation speaks to us of you, Lord, and of your Son through whom you created it. He is the fullness of your self-expression, and shows us the way to you. Let us always be open and sensitive to your Word to us, especially in him.

6

BOTH LORD AND CHRIST

Psalm 110 : 1-4   *"Sit at my right hand"*

The Lord says to my lord:
    "Sit at my right hand,
    till I make your enemies your footstool."
The Lord sends forth from Zion
    your mighty sceptre.
    Rule in the midst of your foes!
Your people will offer themselves freely
    on the day you lead your host
    upon the holy mountains.
From the womb of the morning
    like dew your youth will come to you.

    The Lord has sworn
    and will not change his mind,
"You are a priest for ever
    after the order of Melchizedek."

Acts 2 : 32-36   *Jesus both Lord and Christ*

This Jesus God raised up, and of that we all are witnesses. Being therefore exalted at the right hand of
God, and having received from the Father the promise
of the Holy Spirit, he has poured out this which you
see and hear. For David did not ascend into the heavens;
but he himself says,

'The Lord said to my Lord, Sit at my right hand,
till I make thy enemies a stool for thy feet.'

Let all the house of Israel therefore know assuredly
that God has made him both Lord and Christ, this
Jesus whom you crucified."

Reflection

Psalm 110 was originally an enthronement hymn too,
but Jesus himself points out in the temple that the
terms of it are so exalted that it surpasses David, or for
that matter any purely earthly figure. The Hebrew can
well be translated also 'from the womb before the dawn
I begot you', which hints clearly though poetically at
the existence of the king with God before the creation,
and at his unique relationship with God, who begot him
from the womb. These mysterious terms will have
helped to form Israel's expectation of the Messiah,
preparing them for the fact that he would be more than
a mere son of David, an earthly ruler and the Lord's
anointed and special representative on earth.

The reason, however, why this psalm is so frequently
quoted or alluded to in the New Testament is the
second line, 'Sit at my right hand'. This is used, as in
our passage from the Acts, to describe the exaltation of
Christ at the resurrection 'to the right hand of the
Father'. The pictorial image is of a heavenly court in
which Christ is enthroned beside his Father — but it
is one of those biblical expressions which has been
assimilated into the English language, and is too familiar
to need a gloss. The same idea is expressed at the end
of Matthew's gospel with 'All power in heaven and on
earth has been given to me.'

The fascination of these sayings is that they show
that the incarnation was real. Before the resurrection

and exaltation Christ did not enjoy the totality of power which now makes him Lord, for if he had done so his exaltation would be meaningless. And yet he was God, and both could and did work miracles which only God could do. This is the basic paradox of the incarnation: how Jesus was man in such a way that his mind and all his powers were human, and yet his person was divine and transfused his human powers to such an extent that he could work divine miracles. And yet on the other side there was still room for him to be transformed at the resurrection, and be given the fullness of power and jurisdiction in a way in which he did not have it beforehand. However this is possible, it is the ground of our hope, for we too will be transformed at the resurrection. We will not, to be sure, receive the power and jurisdiction which are his, but we shall, following him, be transformed from earthly bodies into spiritual ones.

Prayer

Lord, you have been exalted at the right hand of God and now, as a man from among men, you hold sway over the whole universe. Guide us to follow you so that we may perfectly submit to your rule and be raised with you to the Father's presence.

7

THE RESTORATION OF PEACE

Isaiah 7:10-17 *A sign in time of distress*

Again the Lord spoke to Ahaz, "Ask a sign of the Lord
your God; let it be deep as Sheol or high as heaven."
But Ahaz said, "I will not ask, and I will not put the
Lord to the test." And he said, "Hear then, O house
of David! Is it too little for you to weary men, that
you weary my God also? Therefore the Lord himself
will give you a sign. Behold, a young woman shall
conceive and bear a son, and shall call his name
Immanuel. He shall eat curds and honey when he
knows how to refuse the evil and choose the good. For
before the child knows how to refuse the evil and
choose the good, the land before whose two kings you
are in dread will be destroyed. The Lord will bring
upon you and upon your people and upon your father's
house such days as have not come since the day that
Ephraim departed from Judah — the king of Assyria."

Matthew 1:18-23 *Emmanuel — God with us*

Now the birth of Jesus Christ took place in this way.
When his mother Mary had been betrothed to Joseph,
before they came together she was found to be with
child of the Holy Spirit; and her husband Joseph, being
a just man and unwilling to put her to shame, resolved
to send her away quietly. But as he considered this,

33

C

behold, an angel of the Lord appeared to him in a dream, saying, "Joseph, son of David, do not fear to take Mary your wife, for that which is conceived in her is of the Holy Spirit; she will bear a son, and you shall call his name Jesus, for he will save his people from their sins." All this took place to fulfil what the Lord had spoken by the prophet:

"Behold, a virgin shall conceive and bear a son,
    and his name shall be called Emmanuel"
(which means, God with us).

Reflection

In the darkest days of Israel's history, when invasion threatened and seemed inevitable, Isaiah promised the birth of a child who would grow up in peace and prosperity, and who would — by his name — symbolise the presence of God with his people. The original Hebrew of Isaiah does not promise that he will be born of a virgin, for 'young woman' does not imply this; but the translations of the Bible into Greek, two centuries before Christ, used the word — as the passage from Matthew shows — which can only have that meaning. The promise is fulfilled in the birth of Jesus from Mary, for then indeed God is with us. Over the gospel of Matthew arches this double promise of the presence of God among men, for it also ends with the word of the risen Christ 'I am with you always', a guarantee which is specifically connected with the continuance of the Church in the world.

In Isaiah the context of the child is peace, the restoration of the perfect peace of Eden. This is part of the longing for peace which is so prominent in the Bible, and forms an important element in the expectation of the Messiah. Palestine was such a strife-torn land, at the centre of the struggle between Egypt and Mesopotamia, trampled on ceaselessly by rival armies of the great powers, that peace was a gift for which they longed with all their heart. The kingdom of God which was to come with the Messiah was to be a kingdom of peace, and the Messiah himself a Prince of Peace. This consisted not only in absence of war and disturbance, but in a total harmony symbolised by the harmony of the beasts described by Isaiah. The harmony which the kingdom of God brings (and this really means the becoming-king of God, when his rule is accepted by men) excludes the rivalry of all creatures, even those naturally hostile to each other. What is meant is that the rivalry and struggles between men, which are so much an ingrained part of our world, will cease; there is to be no self-aggrandisement or jealousy, nor any of the other causes of dissension.

The presence of God among men is no static thing like the presence of a block of wood in a room. It is the presence of something active which has effect on the whole world, and a prime effect is the spread of the reign of God among men in harmony and peace. This is a particular in which it is easy for us to see that the reign of God has a long way to go before it is complete and fulfilled.

Prayer

Lord Jesus Christ, you are God with us. We lay ourselves open to you. Bring us the peace within ourselves which is so essential a part of your kingdom, and help us to spread it among men.

8

LIGHT IN THE DARKNESS

Isaiah 9:2-3 *The people who walked in darkness*

The people who walked in darkness
    have seen a great light;
those who dwelt in a land of deep darkness,
    on them has light shined.
Thou hast multiplied the nation,
    thou hast increased its joy;
they rejoice before thee
    as with joy at the harvest,
    as men rejoice when they divide the spoil.

Luke 2:25-32 *A light to the Gentiles*

Now there was a man in Jerusalem, whose name was
Simeon, and this man was righteous and devout, looking for the consolation of Israel, and the Holy Spirit
was upon him. And it had been revealed to him by the
Holy Spirit that he should not see death before he had
seen the Lord's Christ. And inspired by the Spirit he
came into the temple; and when the parents brought
in the child Jesus, to do for him according to the custom
of the law, he took him up in his arms and blessed God
and said,
"Lord, now lettest thou thy servant depart in peace,
    according to thy word;

for mine eyes have seen thy salvation
which thou hast prepared
    in the presence of all peoples,
a light for revelation to the Gentiles,
and for glory to thy people Israel."

Reflection

Light is such a universal image of hope and relief from
strain, fear or depression that it needs no comment.
The darkness and gloom of sin and bondage are to be
dispelled by the light of God's messenger. Simeon sees
that this light is to spread also to the non-Jewish peoples,
who traditionally among the Jews were considered to be
benighted and wrapped in impenetrable darkness. It
was a great break-through in the appreciation of God's
love for all men to realize that his care and salvation
were destined for all nations, not only the Jews.

But in biblical terms the image of light was acquired
more than its general significance; it has particular
connotations too. God himself is described in terms of
dazzling, inaccessible light. In the visions of God his
presence is made known by fire or light, as at the
burning bush or in the great opening vision of Ezekiel
when he appears concealed in flashing fire. In many
visions of the prophets, too, and in the conversion of
Saul it is blinding light which intimates God's presence.
The light of God is, then, the revelation of God and
his presence. When light comes to the gentiles it is God
himself who is given to them. Christ as the light is God.
In Northern climates it is perhaps only the awesome
power of the lightning which gives us an image of
sufficient intensity, but in the desert the concentrated,

fierce and uncompromising glare of the inescapable light can give a frightening experience of God.

As so many images of God, then, light is a two-edged weapon. Light gives security, knowledge, confidence, warmth. But it is also possible to be afraid of the light, for it is searching and often reveals what we would prefer to leave unseen. God's light searches the depths of the heart, and we may prefer to shun the light rather than allow ourselves to see in his light some of the darker corners of our being. To come to the light of Christ we need a certain purity and sincerity, an ability to face ourselves.

For Paul there is a further dimension of this image of light. In 2 Corinthians he compares the two covenants: the first revelation of Sinai was accompanied by such brightness that Moses' face thereafter had to remain veiled; but the brightness of the new covenant far exceeds this. This light 'has shone in our hearts to give the light of the knowledge of the glory of God in the face of Christ' (2 Cor. 5:6), and a little earlier he says that we are being transformed into the likeness of him whom we behold. There is a communication of this light, and if we remain open and faithful to it we are transformed gradually into the light of Christ.

Prayer

Lord, light of the world, you shine in the darkness and the darkness cannot comprehend you, for your light is penetrating, firm and uncompromising. Give us the courage and objectivity to come and stand before your light, that we may see our shadows and you may dispel them.

9

UNTO US A CHILD IS BORN

Isaiah 9:6-7   *To us a child is born*

For to us a child is born,
   to us a son is given;
and the government will be upon his shoulder,
   and his name will be called
"Wonderful Counsellor, Mighty God,
   Everlasting Father, Prince of Peace."
Of the increase of his government and of peace
   there will be no end,
upon the throne of David, and over his kingdom,
   to establish it, and to uphold it
with justice and with righteousness
   from this time forth and for evermore.
The zeal of the Lord of hosts will do this.

Reflection

The culmination of the promise of Isaiah to Ahaz when
Jerusalem was threatened by invasion contains terms
which are stunning if they are to be understood literally.
Even 'mighty God' need not strictly be understood, it
is true, of God being born on earth, for the Hebrews
were used to the idea of divine figures in the surrounding
nations, and so could understand the word normally

reserved by them for Yahweh also of lesser, heroic figures; so it can be used also of the mighty ones of the earth, powerful and highly respected, but mortal. Nevertheless its natural and obvious sense, when it is not given some special qualification like 'the gods *of the land*', is of the Lord God, and it would suggest the paradox of the incarnation. Similarly 'eternal father' would naturally suggest God, for God is called father of his people, and eternity and unchangingness are associated — particularly in the unstable and changeable world of the time — especially with God.

The other two double titles do not so clearly suggest that the child will be God; but they contain within themselves a great yearning. For a hundred and fifty years when this prophecy was made, the surrounding countries had been torn by strife and constantly threatened with devastation. Neighbours and great powers had made war, leaving Judah feeling isolated and unprotected. Above all, recently the might of Assyria had grown and she was gradually eating up all the little states to the North, working ever nearer, and enslaving the inhabitants. Amidst all this the counsels of Judah were uncertain and divided. Hence the longing at this stage for a Wonderful Counsellor and Prince of Peace who would bring certainty and direction and stability to the wavering and perilous course of Israel's history. We can see this longing fulfilled perfectly in the peace of the Kingdom, ruled by Christ, and in his gift of the Counsellor-Spirit, the sure guide on whom we can rely.

Some reflection, however, is not out of place on the wider implications of the other titles. We are so used to the fact of the incarnation that we easily forget how virtually impossible it is, and the shock it brings to anyone with an exalted idea of God. Apart from our attempt to create a God after our own image and like-ness — an old man with a long beard — the creator of the universe, so limitless in time and space, can never be brought down to our level. It is incredible that this creator should restrict himself to any humanity. Even the personal qualities we know in men which we attribute to God, such as love and knowledge, exist in him in such a different mode that one can almost say our statements are meaningless. It is not surprising that, until the incarnation really occurred, even God's revelation could do no more than hint at it obscurely, for anything clearer would have seemed total madness or blasphemy.

Prayer

Lord, through your prophets you hinted at the unbelievable truth of your generosity. Help us in believing that you became man to penetrate more the depths of your love for us, and not to lose the sense of your infinite greatness.

10

THE SPIRIT OF THE LORD

Isaiah 11:1-5   *The gifts of the Spirit*

There shall come forth a shoot
    from the stump of Jesse,
and a branch shall grow out of his roots.
And the Spirit of the Lord shall rest upon him,
    the spirit of wisdom and understanding,
    the spirit of counsel and might,
    the spirit of knowledge and the fear of the Lord.
And his delight shall be in the fear of the Lord.

He shall not judge by what his eyes see,
    or decide by what his ears hear;
but with righteousness he shall judge the poor,
    and decide with equity for the meek of the earth;
and he shall smite the earth with the rod of his mouth,
    and with the breath of his lips
        he shall slay the wicked.
Righteousness shall be the girdle of his waist,
    and faithfulness the girdle of his loins.

Reflection

The Isaiah passage is that from which the traditional
seven gifts of the Spirit are taken, though of course
it is originally meant of the Messiah. The doctrine of the

Holy Spirit as a separate divine person had not yet begun to appear, and the spirit is thought of very much as God's activity in the world, God's means of giving special power to men for a particular purpose, and his communication of himself to this end. The Hebrew lack of adjectives means that what we would express as 'a wise and understanding spirit', and so on, is expressed by a noun, 'a spirit of wisdom and understanding'. Such will be the spirit of the Messiah, and each of these qualities has in the Hebrew an awesome and numinous aura because it is used basically of the qualities of God.

His wisdom is the inscrutable, unfathomable abyss which is so far beyond man's understanding that man can, like Solomon, only pray for a superficial touch of it, or can, like Job, only stammer incomprehension and submission when confronted by it. His understanding is the perfect, effortless knowledge by which he knows and supremely judges the inmost depths of all things, so that concealment or pretence are ludicrous; not only does he 'know what is in man', but holds in his understanding the nature of all things as their creator and master. With the spirit of counsel and might we move more into the sphere of the human, but still where it is God's working directly on man that is immediately perceived. The spirit of counsel is that of the sagacious adviser to the king, the canny wit and statecraft which is so much valued among the Semites. It is not only a shrewdness and ability to get things through, but — and here the godlike quality enters — a serene command of the scene and a lucid control of its complexities. The spirit of might is that of a warrior, a massive and mighty fighter, and perhaps even more of the mighty unknown figure who stands behind them and whose might is made known in the thunder and lightning of the mountains and the merciless control of the monstrous deep.

All these divine qualities will go to compose the spirit of the Messiah; they will be his breath and so his life-principle; everything he does will be intinct with them. But they will be unified and directed by another quality — and it is here that the human aspect of the Messiah comes in, as he is face to face with God. The fear of the Lord is not terror, for perfect love drives out fear, but an awe and reverence which suffuses the whole being, before the unapproachable and unsoundable being in which these qualities find their fullest meaning.

Prayer

O God, in you above all are found wisdom and understanding, counsel, might and knowledge. In your Son's mysterious nature are these qualities combined with awe and respect for you as God and Father. Grant that we, the members of his body, may join him in sharing these your qualities.

11

THE MERCY OF GOD

Isaiah 42:1-4   *The Servant of the Lord*

Behold my servant, whom I uphold,
  my chosen, in whom my soul delights;
I have put my Spirit upon him,
  he will bring forth justice to the nations.
He will not cry or lift up his voice,
  or make it heard in the street;
a bruised reed he will not break,
  and a dimly burning wick he will not quench;
  he will faithfully bring forth justice.
He will not fail or be discouraged
  till he has established justice in the earth;
  and the coastlands wait for his law.

Luke 4:16-22   *Jesus at Nazareth*

And he came to Nazareth, where he had been brought
up; and he went to the synagogue, as his custom was,
on the sabbath day. And he stood up to read; and there
was given to him the book of the prophet Isaiah. He
opened the book and found the place where it was
written,

"The Spirit of the Lord is upon me,
  because he has anointed me to preach
    good news to the poor.

D

He has sent me to proclaim release to the captives
and recovering of sight to the blind,
to set at liberty those who are oppressed,
to proclaim the acceptable year of the Lord."

And he closed the book, and gave it back to the
attendant, and sat down; and the eyes of all in the
synagogue were fixed on him. And he began to say to
them, "Today this scripture has been fulfilled in your
hearing." And all spoke well of him, and wondered at
the gracious words which proceeded out of his mouth;
and they said, "Is not this Joseph's son?"

Reflection

The Isaiah passage sings of a servant of the Lord, his
messenger who will fulfil his plan for the earth, a
mysterious figure who seems sometimes to be identified
with Israel, sometimes merely associated with but
differentiated from Israel as a whole. The point here is
that he brings the mercy and gentleness of God. These
are the qualities, the essential nature of God, which
Yahweh proclaimed to be his when, after the people had
revolted and broken the first covenant in the desert, he
revealed himself to Moses, passing before him and crying
'Yahweh, Yahweh, a God merciful and gracious, slow
to anger, and abounding in steadfast love and faithful-
ness' (Exodus 34:6). This was the first revelation of
the meaning of the mysterious name of Yahweh, the
aspect of his nature which he chose to make known first
to man, the impression which he wished to be deepest
engraved in man's image of God. When man sins it is
always this aspect that comes to the fore as God's
response, the automatic reaction of his love for man,
calling him back with the open arms of affection.

Luke is the evangelist of God's mercy, and he alone gives us this inaugural sermon of Jesus in the synagogue at Nazareth, making this the keynote of Jesus' whole mission. But this emphasis is visible in so many of Jesus' parables and so many of his clashes with the Pharisees. It was to captives that he came, to the sick who needed a physician. While the people who were known to be religious and thought to be the favoured of God strove to gain their own justification by exact and hard obedience to the myriad demands of the Law, Jesus made straight for sinners. His company was with outcasts such as tax-collectors, men ostracised from the worshipping community, their employment made them odious not only on the natural plane (as are all who fleece people of their money), but also on the religious plane, since they had sold themselves to the pagan Romans. Morally they were, so to speak, displaced persons, unattached and friendless. Presumably they had given up trying to seek God, and most of them would have been pretty hard-bitten. And yet their reaction is, again and again in the gospels, enthusiastic; one can almost see the light spark in the eye and feel the unexpected yearning kindle in the heart of a Matthew or a Zacchaeus as they realize that the mercy of God has been brought specially to them by this man Jesus, that they have been singled out.

So it is not the unloving drudgery of conscientious observance which invites Christ; it is the ready and generous response to the sudden call. This is not to say that routine observance is condemned — nor were the Pharisees condemned for this. But routine is composed of a series of individual calls by Christ, as when he passed before Matthew's customs-table at the roadside. Even if we are hopeless and know that we are hopeless, he is waiting for the willing response of the glad light in the eyes.

Prayer

Lord, at times we are hopeless sinners, at times just apathetic and unresponsive. Make me aware that it is you, with your glance of mercy, who are calling to me so often, and draw me to follow you.

12

THE GOOD SHEPHERD

Ezekiel 34:11-16, 23   *God will shepherd his people*

For thus says the Lord God: "Behold, I, I myself will search for my sheep, and will seek them out. As a shepherd seeks out his flock when some of his sheep have been scattered abroad, so will I seek out my sheep; and I will rescue them from all places where they have been scattered on a day of clouds and thick darkness. And I will bring them out from the peoples, and gather them from the countries, and will bring them into their own land; and I will feed them on the mountains of Israel, by the fountains, and in all the inhabited places of the country. I will feed them with good pasture, and upon the mountain heights of Israel shall be their pasture; there they shall lie down in good grazing land, and on fat pasture they shall feed on the mountains of Israel. I myself will be the shepherd of my sheep, and I will make them lie down, says the Lord God. I will seek the lost, and I will bring back the strayed, and I will bind up the crippled, and I will strengthen the weak, and the fat and the strong I will watch over; I will feed them in justice.... And I will set up over them one shepherd, my servant David, and he shall feed them; he shall feed them and be their shepherd."

So Jesus again said to them, "Truly, truly, I say to you, I am the door of the sheep. All who came before me are thieves and robbers; but the sheep did not heed them... The thief comes only to steal and kill and destroy; I came that they may have life, and have it abundantly. I am the good shepherd. The good shepherd lays down his life for the sheep. He who is a hireling and not a shepherd, whose own the sheep are not, sees the wolf coming and leaves the sheep and flees; and the wolf snatches them and scatters them. He flees because he is a hireling and cares nothing for the sheep. I am the good shepherd; I know my own and my own know me, as the Father knows me and I know the Father; and I lay down my life for the sheep."

Reflection

One sometimes wonders how Palestinian sheep pass the time; there is no luscious green grass to munch as in our rich climate. They wander over the baked and sandy hills, snatching at an occasional tuft of dusty grass. The shepherd boy has a very real job, watching that they do not stray out into the wilderness or get stuck in a crevasse, ready to rescue them and repel — this more in former days — robbers or wild beasts from the forests above the Jordan. Situations of real danger can arise.

So when God promises in Ezekiel that he will pasture his sheep where they can lie down in good grazing land and on fat pasture he is promising something idyllic, especially for the rocky and boulder-strewn hills of Israel. The security and reassurance of having God himself as a shepherd is all the greater by contrast with those who had recently had charge of the flock, rulers who had been concerned only with their own advantage, and had themselves harried rather than cherished and protected the flock. He provides even the climate and physical conditions which his people desire, but this picture is primarily an image of constant, unbroken, loving care, of whole-hearted attention and devotion.

Jesus could find no better image of his selflessness. There is no question of the sentimentality of soft, woolly sheep; a shepherd's is a hard and unremitting task. He is well aware that in taking this title for himself he is accepting to fulfil Old Testament figures: in Isaiah 40 the shepherd to come is the type of absolute devotion and tender care. By reference to Ezekiel Jesus claims not only to bring the blissful times of the renewal of the world to comfort Israel, but also that he is in the place of God, for it was God himself who was to come and pasture his flock. Yet also only just below the surface is the thought of the suffering which his role is to bring; care for others always exposes one to suffering and perhaps especially in this sort of concern.

It is worth dwelling on the sheep too. The parable is probably not intended as an allegory, so too much stress should not be laid on the comparison of ourselves to sheep; but it is at least partly present through the job the shepherd has. Sheep are not cuddly creatures, at any rate sheep of the wilderness are not. They are awkward to deal with, easily startled and apt to shy off in the wrong direction, after which it requires a lot of patience to coax them back. Particularly, they will follow a leader off against all good sense, recklessly and stubbornly. Christ has to deal with a number of these faults in ourselves. We forget his love and concern for us; startled and alarmed by things we cannot understand, we bolt away from his protection and guidance. Too easily we are deflected by a trend or strong influence

55

or merely human respect, and bone-headedly rush towards disaster. There was, I think, some humour in Jesus' parable of the Good Shepherd.

Prayer

Keep a watchful eye on us, Lord, silly sheep as we are. And, as you watch over us, let us be aware that you are a shepherd who is prepared to give his life for his sheep.

13

THE REFINER'S FIRE

Malachi 3 : 1-3   *Who can endure the day of his coming?*

Behold, I send my messenger to prepare the way before
me, and the Lord whom you seek will suddenly come
to his temple; the messenger of the covenant in whom
you delight, behold, he is coming, says the Lord of hosts.
But who can endure the day of his coming, and who
can stand when he appears?

For he is like a refiner's fire and like fullers' soap;
he will sit as a refiner and purifier of silver, and he will
purify the sons of Levi and refine them like gold and
silver, till they present right offerings to the Lord.

Matthew 3 : 7-12   *The Baptist's threat*

But when he saw many of the Pharisees and Sadducees
coming for baptism, he said to them, "You brood of
vipers! Who warned you to flee from the wrath to
come? Bear fruit that befits repentance, and do not
presume to say to yourselves, 'We have Abraham as
our father'; for I tell you, God is able from these stones
to raise up children to Abraham. Even now the axe is
laid to the root of the trees; every tree therefore that
does not bear good fruit is cut down and thrown into
the fire.

"I baptize you with water for repentance, but he
who is coming after me is mightier than I, whose sandals

I am not worthy to carry; he will baptize you with the Holy Spirit and with fire. His winnowing fork is in his hand, and he will clear his threshing floor and gather his wheat into the granary, but the chaff he will burn with unquenchable fire."

Reflection

There is another side to the coming of Christ than gentleness and tenderness, which causes the prophet to ask who can endure the day of his coming. The Baptist too uses this image of fire as a refining agent, purging away all the base alloy and leaving only the pure metal, but he piles one image on top of another to stress that this is the moment of division: the axe at the root of the useless tree, the winnowing fork used by a farmer to separate the grain from the chaff (as both are tossed together in the air, the lighter chaff is caught by the wind and blown further than the heavier grain, so that they fall in different heaps).

In spite of his love there is a fierceness and uncompromisingness about Jesus which are terrifying: 'sell all you have and follow me . . . leave the dead to bury their dead . . . I have not come to bring peace but a sword . . . he who does not take his cross and follow me is not worthy of me." The refiner's fire was to operate the great divide between those who accept him and those who neglect or reject him. It was a crisis which shook all who came into contact with him from their ways of comfortable mediocrity. An instant decision was needed, the person judged and was judged.

But it is the same with us. Confronted with the decision of Christ we have to choose. After that the fire does not just destroy the chaff but refines the metal — the fire not of hell but of purgatory. Once the decision is made we have to be gradually refined and tested, more deeply as we become stronger metal. The idea that we might be caught out suddenly by the arrival of death and plunged into the fires of perdition is an unworthy superstition — unworthy of God's fidelity — for life is a process of gradual hardening in good or in evil, of fixing into a mould, and God must take this seriously. The 'fires' of purgatory are only an image of the testing and refining process, which must continue if it is unfinished in this life.

Christ came to spread fire upon the earth, and was impatient that it be kindled. He was to baptize in the Holy Spirit and in fire. Besides being a purifying and refining agent fire is associated with the consummation of the world, the final cataclysm which brings in the completion of the kingdom and the perfect rule of God. It was in this sense primarily that Malachi and the Baptist thought of fire, for they were expecting God's messenger to usher in, then and there, the restored and purified world. But one can say that we, baptized in fire, are the agents of God in bringing about the completion of the kingdom. The tongues of fire which rested on the Twelve at Pentecost mark them out as belonging already to God's final kingdom; so we too by spreading the fire of the gospel help in the kindling of that fire for which Christ longed.

Prayer

O God, make us true metal by purging away with your fire all our imperfections. Grant us the strength not to flinch before your testing and to realize that these trials are the proof of your love for us.

14

THE MIRROR OF GOD

Wisdom 7:22-81   *The wisdom of God*

For in wisdom there is a spirit that is intelligent, holy,
unique, manifold, subtle,
mobile, clear, unpolluted,
distinct, invulnerable, loving the good, keen,
irresistible, beneficent, humane,
steadfast, sure, free from anxiety,
all-powerful, overseeing all,
and penetrating through all spirits
that are intelligent and pure and most subtle.
For wisdom is more mobile than any motion;
because of her pureness she pervades
    and penetrates all things.
For she is a breath of the power of God,
and a pure emanation of the glory of the Almighty;
therefore nothing defiled gains entrance into her.
For she is a reflection of eternal light,
a spotless mirror of the working of God,
and an image of his goodness.
Though she is but one, she can do all things,
and while remaining in herself, she renews all things;
in every generation she passes into holy souls
and makes them friends of God, and prophets;
for God loves nothing so much as
    the man who lives with wisdom.
For she is more beautiful than the sun,

and excels every constellation of the stars.
Compared with the light she is found to be superior,
for it is succeeded by the night,
but against wisdom evil does not prevail.
She reaches mightily from one end
    of the earth to the other,
and she orders all things well.

Colossians 1:13-20   *A hymn to Christ*

He has delivered us from the dominion of darkness and transferred us to the kingdom of his beloved Son, in whom we have redemption, the forgiveness of sins.

He is the image of the invisible God, the first-born of all creation; for in him all things were created, in heaven and on earth, visible and invisible, whether thrones or dominions or principalities or authorities — all things were created through him and for him. He is before all things, and in him all things hold together. He is the head of the body, the church; he is the beginning, the first-born from the dead, that in every-thing he might be pre-eminent. For in him all the fullness of God was pleased to dwell, and through him to reconcile to himself all things, whether on earth or in heaven, making peace by the blood of his cross.

Reflection

In giving the picture of the Wisdom of God in the Old Testament the author is attempting to describe how wisdom, the mysterious factor in the world which makes everything make sense, is associated with God. He starts from experience of this manifold power which is so sensitively and richly described at the beginning of the passage; then he rises to the explanation and origin of it in God, and finally returns again to earth, with the beneficent presence of wisdom in the world, among men. The core of the passage, then, is where the author is using image after image to try to describe how wisdom is, yet is not, God.

It is because of this relationship of wisdom to God that Christ is sometimes described in the New Testament as the wisdom of God. There is perhaps, even in the later elaborations of Christian theology, no better way of trying to express the impossible than by these images of continuity, identity and yet distinction. To the ancients, perhaps primitively, an image or statue was thought of as somehow possessing the character of the original; it was not merely a poor substitute, but made the person present, could be honoured or insulted; the same mentality is behind the sympathetic magic of harming a person by sticking pins into or burning his waxen image. So the image of his goodness somehow makes his goodness present in the world.

Similarly the two images of light are trying to express a mysterious extension, a making present of the original. Is the reflection of a light the light itself? Does a perfect, spotless mirror give back the original itself? At least to a practical, not highly sophisticated mind, it may seem so. And at the same time there is the idea of continuity and total dependence: take away the light and there is no reflection; take away the original and there is nothing reflected in the mirror.

The breath of the power of God is itself the power of God. The metaphor cannot be taken literally, for power has no breath; but to the Hebrew the breath is the life, and life departs from a living body with its last breath. So the breath of God's power is a way of describing the essence or the inner reality of God's power. One of the primary ways in which this power manifested itself was in creation; this was when his light shone, when his working and his goodness together produced the world; this was when his wisdom was at work.

God's wisdom is, then, the way prepared in the Old Testament for characterising the Second Person of the Trinity. He was always with God and of God, possessing all the divine characteristics which make God beyond human reach, barely describable in human vocabulary, reflecting God in all things. To emphasise his superiority to the world (since some people at Colossae compared Christ to created powers) Paul stresses that he is above creation, and that, as Wisdom, he is the principle and power by which God acted in creation.

Prayer

Your image, Lord, and the mirror of your power is for ever with you. Through him you created the world and yet he became man for our sakes, and unites himself to us in human nature and in the Church. Let us return love for this love.

15

THE SON GIVES LIFE

Deuteronomy 32:39 *God's total command of the world*

See now that I, even I, am he,
and there is no god beside me;
I kill and I make alive;
I wound and I heal;
and there is none that can deliver out of my hand.

John 5:19-21 *The Son works as the Father*

Jesus said to them, "Truly, truly, I say to you, the Son can do nothing of his own accord, but only what he sees the Father doing; for whatever he does, that the Son does likewise. For the Father loves the Son, and shows him all that he himself is doing; and greater works than these will he show him, that you may marvel. For as the Father raises the dead and gives them life, so also the Son gives life to whom he will."

Reflection

The passage from Deuteronomy is an awesome expression of God's utter and complete control of men; our lives lie in his hand, dependent on his whim. It is also a semitic way of expressing by the extremes all that lies between: if God can kill and make alive, this is a way of saying that he can do all that lies between these two, that he has total command of us in all our movements.

The blasphemy by Jesus which so outraged the Jews in the temple was that he claimed for himself this same power of giving life. Life was sacred to God, and only he controlled it; this was a basic tenet of Judaism, recognized in every sacrifice, where the blood, symbolising the animal's life, belongs to God alone. And here is a man who claims exactly this divine power to raise the dead and give them life. Nor was this all. Jesus claims to imitate God, whom he calls simply 'the Father', in all he does. By this he is implying a uniquely close relationship. The meaning of 'the Son' and the relationship implied to God is not immediately clear in itself, for the Jews had never envisaged that God could have a son like himself; they would automatically understand it as a claim to a specially close relationship indeed, but one such as Moses or Israel (also called 'son of God') enjoyed. But Jesus shatters this interpretation, bold enough though it was. The picture of the Son watching the Father and doing what he does, must have recalled the Hebrew law that a father must teach his son his trade or craft; it is as though the Son is apprenticed to the Father, with the same skills as he but working always in accordance with the Father's plans, watching the Father's every move. It is a picture of the most perfect close family harmony and equality with reverent obedience. It is not the obedience which was shocking but the quality.

The semitic mind thinks in terms not of natures but of actions, so that someone is described in terms of what he can do; his capacities define his nature. So when Jesus claims to share the action of God, in particular the power and control of God over the life of man, in the way a respectful son shares his father's craft, then he is making a far fuller claim than when he just says that God is his Father. To the Western mind too, however, the statement that Father and Son have the same nature is cold and abstract. It means far more that the Son should have the powers which are God's alone, the absolute control over life, to give it and take it away, the awesome power of ultimate judgment, the power of wisdom or knowledge itself, by which he makes the intelligibility of things and gives the universe its logic. These supreme powers he exercises only in accordance with the Father's will, so that at the same time there is the most unlimited freedom and the most total subjection. This is the meaning of the union of wills of Father and Son, the most perfect obedience.

Prayer

Lord Jesus, all-powerful as you are, you watch the Father to do his will, like a son in the father's workshop. Help me to imitate your respectful love and to abandon petty self-assertiveness that I may follow your divine way.

16

THE LIMITATIONS OF JESUS

Luke 2:41-52 *The child Jesus grows up*

Now his parents went to Jerusalem every year at the feast of the Passover. And when he was twelve years old, they went up according to custom; and when the feast was ended, as they were returning, the boy Jesus stayed behind in Jerusalem. His parents did not know it, but supposing him to be in the company they went a day's journey, and they sought him among their kinsfolk and acquaintances; and when they did not find him, they returned to Jerusalem, seeking him. After three days they found him in the temple, sitting among the teachers, listening to them and asking them questions; and all who heard him were amazed at his understanding and his answers. And when they saw him they were astonished; and his mother said to him, "Son, why have you treated us so? Behold, your father and I have been looking for you anxiously." And he said to them, "How is it that you sought me? Did you not know that I must be in my Father's house?" And they did not understand the saying which he spoke to them. And he went down with them and came to Nazareth, and was obedient to them; and his mother kept all these things in her heart.

And Jesus increased in wisdom and in stature, and in favour with God and man.

But of that day or that hour no one knows, not even the angels in heaven, nor the Son, but only the Father.

Reflection

A Christian believes that God became truly man, and we accept that he was at one time a helpless baby, physically dependent on his mother, and that he grew to manhood through all the ways of adolescence. This in itself is a comforting thought, to know that Jesus was formed by similar experiences to our own. But is much harder to accept that he really thought as a man thinks, that he really learnt, and so that he was really ignorant. He was God too, and it is too easy to pay lip-service to belief in his humanity without accepting in practice that he had a fully human mind.

We are apt to think that since he was God he must, as a man too, have known everything. It is true that it would be meaningless to assert that Jesus the man was also God unless he was conscious of his divinity, but this does not at all mean that he knew everything. On one level, it is ludicrous to suppose that he knew scientific facts for which not so much as the terms had been evolved; on another, God's knowledge is just not such that a human mind can contain it; he could not know anything as God knows it. So Jesus too experienced the darkness of human ignorance; this was, in a way, the most humiliating limitation which he took upon himself, the greatest proof of his love for us in embracing solidarity with us in the incarnation.

And yet it also opened to him the avenues of human experience which are part of the glory of humanity. If he had known everything he could never have learnt, could never have experienced the joy of achievement in self-development, in discovery, in expanding his universe. By accepting these limitations he made possible the sharing of these positive human experiences too. He learnt gradually what was the will of the Father for himself; in his human mind he learnt about himself, as every child gradually begins to come to self-knowledge but more, for he learnt about God, and in doing so learnt what it was to be God. When he sat at the feet of the doctors of the Law he was not merely mocking them and testing them, showing that he knew all the time. He was learning from them, surprising them by his sharp wits and ready answers, for the knowledge came to him naturally, as it could come to no other. But for all that, he genuinely learnt.

So too with detailed knowledge of the future and of the day of judgment. By his knowledge of God's will, of his own mission and fate (for his knowledge of the scriptures, his union with the Father in prayer and his clear-sighted reading of the reactions to his message must have combined to point the way to his rejection and execution) he knew much of the future events which were to come upon him. But he had no blue-print of the future. In this he had to rely on the Father's will in trust, but lack of knowledge. He shared with us that human limitation — or is it a human dignity? — that he had not the clarity and certainty of what was to happen, but must recognize his dependence on the Father.

Prayer

Lord Jesus, you shared our uncertainty about the future and our reliance on your Father and ours. Only your reliance was absolute and unquestioning. Help me to trust unreservedly in our Father's will for the future.

17

JESUS AS GOD ON THE WATERS

Psalm 107 : 23-30   *God's mastery of the seas*

Some went down to the sea in ships,
     doing business on the great waters;
they saw the deeds of the Lord,
     his wondrous works in the deep.
For he commanded, and raised the stormy wind,
     which lifted up the waves of the sea.
They mounted up to heaven, they
          went down to the depths;
     their courage melted away in their evil plight;
they reeled and staggered like drunken men,
     and were at their wits' end.
Then they cried to the Lord in their trouble,
     and he delivered them from their distress;
he made the storm be still,
     and the waves of the sea were hushed.
Then they were glad because they had quiet,
     and he brought them to their desired haven.

Matthew 14 : 22-33 *Jesus walks on the sea*

Then he made the disciples get into the boat and go
before him to the other side, while he dismissed the
crowds. And after he had dismissed the crowds he went
up into the hills by himself to pray. When evening came,

he was there alone, but the boat by this time was many furlongs distant from the land, beaten by the waves; for the wind was against them. And in the fourth watch of the night he came to them, walking on the sea. But when the disciples saw him walking on the sea, they were terrified, saying, "It is a ghost!" And they cried out for fear. But immediately he spoke to them, saying, "Take heart, it is I; have no fear."

And Peter answered him, "Lord, if it is you, bid me come to you on the water." He said, "Come." So Peter got out of the boat and walked on the water and came to Jesus; but when he saw the wind, he was afraid, and beginning to sink he cried out, "Lord, save me." Jesus immediately reached out his hand and caught him, saying to him, "O man of little faith, why did you doubt?" And when they got into the boat, the wind ceased. And those in the boat worshipped him, saying, "Truly you are the Son of God."

Reflection

In Hebrew thought the sea was a powerful and awesome force over which God alone had control. It was the embodiment of the evil forces of chaos which might return and engulf the world, as they did at the flood, if God did not hold them back. Therefore, as the Psalms show, he alone has mastery over their mighty waves, and he rides serenely in power over them.

This explains the awe of the disciples when they see Jesus walking over the waves to them in the midst of the storm — and storms can be very sudden and severe on the Lake of Galilee, surrounded as it is by high hills — and calming the fury of the storm. In the gospels this incident is placed where the disciples are learning on their own about the true meaning of Jesus.

The crowds have already rejected him, and now he withdraws with his chosen disciples so that at least a small band will come to understand him. But it was difficult work, and they are slow to learn. In Mark's version of this story they are, indeed, astounded at what happens, but they do not yet understand what Jesus is; one sees how little an impression teaching with mere words would have made if such a dramatic and meaningful occurrence only made them wonder. Yet we too are slow to learn by events and to recognize the hand of God in our lives. Looking back on this story we can see its meaning, but that is because we already believe in the divinity of Christ, just as looking back afterwards on an incident in life we can see in it the hand of God. However, their very slowness to believe can remind us again how incredible, almost how impossible, it was that God should become man.

Matthew, in his version of the story, underlines its significance for the sake of his readers by making Peter acknowledge him already as the Son of God, which according to Mark never happened until the centurion at the foot of the cross so acknowledged him. But then Matthew is often concerned to give a more favourable impression of the future leaders of the Church, and somewhat moderates the severe rebukes which they receive from Jesus in Mark. But Matthew shows us freely an attractive weakness of Peter: his impetuosity, as full of enthusiasm he rushes to meet Jesus and then finds his courage fails him.

There are two other significant touches in the story. It is the fourth watch of the night when Jesus appears. They had struggled, seemingly deserted, all through the night, but Jesus waits till they have been thoroughly tested, and when their morale must have been at its lowest ebb, before he comes to save them. The other unforgettable gesture is that of the Saviour, reaching out his hand to rescue Peter as he sinks, a gesture repeated in early Christian art as Christ goes into the underworld after his death and reaches out his hand to draw the dead with him in the triumph of his resurrection.

Prayer

You stretched out your hand from heaven, Lord Jesus, by your incarnation, to draw us when we are floundering back to your side. Give me the faith and confidence to accept your hand, even though I must wait till the fourth watch of the night.

18

THE CHAMPION OF THE AFFLICTED

Isaiah 61 : 1-3   Comfort for those who mourn

The Spirit of the Lord God is upon me,
    because the Lord has anointed me
to bring good tidings to the afflicted;
    he has sent me to bind up the brokenhearted,
to proclaim liberty to the captives,
    and the opening of the prison to
        those who are bound;
to proclaim the year of the Lord's favour,
    and the day of vengeance of our God;
    to comfort all who mourn;
to grant to those who mourn in Zion —
    to give them a garland instead of ashes,
the oil of gladness instead of mourning,
    the mantle of praise instead of a faint spirit;
that they may be called oaks of righteousness,
    the planting of the Lord, that he may be glorified.

Luke 6 : 20-26   The beatitudes

And he lifted up his eyes on his disciples, and said:

"Blessed are you poor, for yours is the kingdom of God.

"Blessed are you that hunger now, for you shall be satisfied.

"Blessed are you that weep now, for you shall laugh.

"Blessed are you when men hate you, and when they exclude you and revile you, and cast out your name as evil, on account of the Son of man! Rejoice in that day, and leap for joy, for behold, your reward is great in heaven; for so their fathers did to the prophets.

"But woe to you that are rich, for you have received your consolation.

"Woe to you that are full now, for you shall hunger.

"Woe to you that laugh now, for you shall mourn and weep.

"Woe to you, when all men speak well of you, for so their fathers did to the false prophets."

Reflection

After the days of Israel's glory as a political power under David and Solomon, as the nation came to be afflicted by one calamity after another, constantly harrassed by one disaster or other, they began to think of themselves as the Poor of Yahweh. A whole theology grew up of suffering and patient dependence on the Lord, acceptance of their lot in the confidence that in all due time the faithful Lord would deliver them. It is this longing which is expressed in the passage of Isaiah.

Then Jesus, in Luke's great sermon, takes as his keynote the deliverance of the afflicted. The beatitudes are subtly different from those of Matthew, for Matthew teaches more the blessedness of certain conditions: 'Blessed are the poor *in spirit*' — a state which will receive its due reward. But Luke promises release and relief from wretchedness; it is a proclamation of liberty for the Poor of Yahweh who have waited so long. A prophet often, if not always, proclaims that the will of the Lord is a dramatic reversal of the present state, that the strong and self-satisfied will receive a rude shock and fall from their eminence, while the Lord, the defender of the weak, will protect and deliver the oppressed. Now Jesus is this prophet who proclaims that there is a reversal. It is not only a reversal of positions of power but a reversal of all scales of value, as the sermon goes on to unfold, where the standards of worldly success and the goals of earthly striving are declared empty. The folly of the Cross is the only wisdom of God.

The two attitudes, shown in Matthew's and Luke's versions of the beatitudes, are of course complementary; we can turn from one to the other as we feel inclined. At almost every moment we are threatened by something or other, and can feel ourselves to be among the classes promised relief by Jesus in these great sayings. Often enough we are actually suffering from poverty in the shape of frustrated desires and needs for material things, or from persecution in the shape of someone's undue failure to recognize our worth and the worth of our ideas. In a way we can always consider ourselves as weeping, for however happy we may be temporarily, this happiness has always some limitation or reservation, at any rate in comparison to the happiness which is promised to us, when all limits to happiness are taken away, and the laughter is truly carefree. So when we feel like this we can look forward to the release which Luke promises.

At other times one may be content with Matthew's version. This is more tranquil, an acceptance of the state not because it is to be reversed but because it is blessed in itself. They are more voluntary restrictions placed upon a person by himself, the blueprint of a Christian attitude. Here Christ is sketching the qualities which go to make up the members of his kingdom.

In both cases, however, we cannot escape the hard truth that the categories accepted by the world are stood on their head by Jesus and his proclamation. If we wish to stand before Jesus — and to see him is to see the Father — we must purge our thoughts and motives pretty radically.

Prayer

Help me to realize, Lord, that your ways are not men's ways, that what the world approves is not necessarily what you approve, that so many goals for which men strive are worthless in your sight. So make me contented with whatever failure or suffering you wish to be mine. Help me to remember always that it is when the horizon is really black that you promise me the kingdom.

19

LEARNING THE FATHER'S WILL

Isaiah 52: 13 - 53: 12   *The suffering Servant of the
    Lord*

Behold, my servant shall prosper,
    he shall be exalted and lifted up,
    and shall be very high.
As many were astonished at him —
    his appearance was so marred,
        beyond human semblance,
    and his form beyond that of the sons of men —
so shall he startle many nations;
    kings shall shut their mouths
        because of him;
for that which has not been told them
    they shall see;
    and that which they have not
        heard they shall understand.
Who has believed what we have heard?
    And to whom has the arm of the
        Lord been revealed?
For he grew up before him like a young plant,
    and like a root out of dry ground;
he had no form of comeliness that
        we should look at him,
    and no beauty that we should desire him.
He was despised and rejected by men;
    a man of sorrows, and acquainted with grief;

F

and as one from whom men hide their faces
    he was despised, and we esteemed him not.
Surely he has borne our griefs
    and carried our sorrows;
yet we esteemed him stricken,
    smitten by God, and afflicted.
But he was wounded for our transgressions,
    he was bruised for our iniquities;
upon him was the chastisement that made us whole,
    and with his stripes we are healed.
All we like sheep have gone astray;
    we have turned every one to his own way;
and the Lord has laid on him
    the iniquity of us all.
He was oppressed, and he was afflicted,
    yet he opened not his mouth;
like a lamb that is led to the slaughter,
    and like a sheep that before its shearers is dumb,
    so he opened not his mouth.
By oppression and judgment he was taken away;
    and as for his generation, who considered
that he was cut off out of the land of the living,
    stricken for the transgression of my people?
And they made his grave with the wicked
    and with a rich man in his death,
although he had done no violence.

Matthew 4:1-11   *The temptations*

Then Jesus was led up by the Spirit into the wilderness to be tempted by the devil. And he fasted forty days and forty nights, and afterward he was hungry. And the tempter came and said to him, "If you are the Son of God, command these stones to become loaves of bread." But he answered, "It is written,
    'Man shall not live by bread alone,
    but by every word that proceeds from
        the mouth of God.'"

Then the devil took him to the holy city, and set him on the pinnacle of the temple, and said to him, "If you are the Son of God, throw yourself down; for it is written,

'He will give his angels charge of you,' and
'On their hands they will bear you up,
lest you strike your foot against a stone.' "

Jesus said to him, "Again it is written, 'You shall not tempt the Lord your God.' " Again, the devil took him to a very high mountain, and showed him all the kingdoms of the world and the glory of them; and he said to him, "All these I will give you, if you will fall down and worship me." Then Jesus said to him, "Begone, Satan! for it is written,

'You shall worship the Lord your God
and him only shall you serve.' "

Then the devil left him, and behold, angels came and ministered to him.

Reflection

As a man Jesus learnt. As God he knew everything, but this omniscient grasp of reality could not enter into his human mind. So he was, as all men, subject to the doubts and uncertainties about the future, about what he should do, about which course he should take. His knowledge that he was God, and his perfect love for and obedience to his Father, did not spare him from the necessity of searching and worrying about what the will of the Father required of him. The gospels record his agony in the garden before his passion as he struggled to steel himself for the ordeal which he knew awaited him, but they tell us less of the agony he must have gone through earlier in deciding his course of life.

To us, now, his mission is clear. But to him, at the time, the course and nature of his work as Messiah was anything but self-evident. There were so many shades of opinion about what the Messiah would be, so many different expectations about the nature of the Kingdom he would bring, that Jesus had to find which was the will of his Father. To make this decision he had the help of the scriptures, the book of God's designs and plans for his people, and prayer. As we see him in the gospels retire often for prayer, and especially before important moments and decisions, so in the hidden period of his preparation he must often have meditated the scriptures, seeking clear guidance, and prayed to his Father. But for him, as for us, there was no magical short cut to a solution; he must search and use the human means with which the Father had endowed him.

The story of the temptations is the dramatic account of this agony of decision at its climax. After his messianic mission had been declared at the baptism he retired to the desert for a final period of preparation and prayer. The three temptations are various ways in which the messianic kingdom was expected which he saw to be false, easy ways out, the suggestions of the devil rather than the will of his Father. One temptation was to provide material good things in plenty — this was the bread, a beginning of the messianic banquet. Another was to perform startling and dazzling miracles which would win him acclaim — throwing himself from the pinnacle of the temple. A third seems to have been political, to expel the Romans and found a world empire — all the kingdoms of the world visible from the high mountain.

But all these are rejected as the ways of the devil, for Jesus' way and the will of his Father are the way of the suffering servant which he knew from Isaiah, the way of suffering and humiliation. This moment of decision and certainty is especially precious, showing how closely Jesus shared our nature and our trials.

Prayer

Lord Jesus, you humbled yourself to share our puzzlement and hesitation, so that we could turn to you for sympathy when we do not know what to do. And finally you chose the path of suffering. Let me not be afraid of the hard decision.

20

THE SON OF MAN

Daniel 7:9-14   *Daniel's vision of heaven*

As I looked,
    thrones were placed
        and one that was ancient of days took his seat;
    his raiment was white as snow,
        and the hair of his head like pure wool;
    his throne was fiery flames,
        its wheels were burning fire.
A stream of fire issued
    and came forth from before him;
a thousand thousands served him,
    and ten thousand times ten
        thousand stood before him;
the court sat in judgment,
    and the books were opened,
... and behold, with the clouds of heaven
    there came one like a son of man,
and he came to the Ancient of Days
    and was presented before him.
And to him was given dominion
    and glory and kingdom,
that all peoples, nations, and languages
    should serve him;
his dominion is an everlasting dominion,
    which shall not pass away,

and his kingdom one
    that shall not be destroyed.

Matthew 24 : 29-31   *The Son of Man gathers his elect*

Immediately after the tribulation of those days the sun
will be darkened, and the moon will not give its light,
and the stars will fall from heaven, and the powers of
the heavens will be shaken; then will appear the sign
of the Son of man in heaven, and then all the tribes
of the earth will mourn, and they will see the Son of
man coming on the clouds of heaven with power and
great glory; and he will send out his angels with a loud
trumpet call, and they will gather his elect from the
four winds, from one end of heaven to the other.

Reflection

It was no use Jesus saying he was God, for this bold
statement simply would not make sense to the Jews
who heard him. They had a sense of the divine far more
exalted and distant than we have — of course, for we
are used to the incarnation which is God coming to be
among us. In the old days they had sung that no people
had its God so close to it as this people, but gradually
the awesomeness of God had become more and more
stressed, at the price of the lessening of the close, warm
relationship between Israel and Yahweh. So God was
infinitely exalted, distant from and other than the world.
But the Jews had also struggled for centuries against
the debased polytheism of the neighbouring peoples and
of their captors in Babylon. Hence they would have
immediately suspected any claim from Jesus that he
was God of being a deviation derived from these reli-
gions. Nor does the New Testament itself call Jesus

God more than a couple of times, in passages written very late.

Instead, Jesus called himself the Son of Man. This was a deliberately mysterious title, for Jesus preferred to force nobody, but rather to drop hints and leave those who would to draw their own conclusions. He called but did not force anyone to follow; he revealed, but in such a way that a response and goodwill were necessary before the truth could sink in. He was the most tactful of teachers, making no assault upon the free will of his hearers. The expression 'Son of Man' could be taken to mean no more than 'man', showing the generic nature of the person, more or less like 'member of the human race', and as such has no remarkable quality at all. But to those who not only heard but also listened it would recall the scene of Daniel.

The scene is the heavenly court, where the Father gives power to a representative of men, power beyond any earthly rule, embracing not only all nations but all time as well, the sort of power which in the earlier messianic hope had been attributed to God himself when he came at the end of days to complete his rule on earth and subdue all creation to his sway. The son of man in this prophecy was a representative of Israel, drawn from the saints, or chosen, of the Most High, perhaps even representing the people as a whole. Jesus, in taking the title as his own, therefore hints that he is this godlike figure who receives God's own power and dominion over the world.

In the gospel passage of Matthew we are reading also a promise of deliverance, for Daniel too was promising deliverance from persecution by the Son of Man. This discourse of Matthew gives the promises of Jesus for the future of his Church: whatever hardships they have to undergo, the Son of Man will finally set them free and establish them in his kingdom and the kingdom of his Father.

Prayer

Lord, even your apostles took a long time to recognize your true dignity. We too are slow to believe and slow to assimilate this belief into the fibre of our lives. You respect us and love us so much that you will not force us. Help me to learn more and more what your godhead must mean to me in my life, who the Son of Man is.

21

THE JUDGMENT OF THE SON

Matthew 25:31-46 *The sheep and the goats*

"When the Son of man comes in his glory, and all the angels with him, then he will sit on his glorious throne. Before him will be gathered all the nations, and he will separate them one from another as a shepherd separates the sheep from the goats, and he will place the sheep at his right hand, but the goats at the left. Then the King will say to those at his right hand, 'Come, O blessed of my Father, inherit the kingdom prepared for you from the foundation of the world; for I was hungry and you gave me food, I was thirsty and you gave me drink, I was a stranger and you welcomed me, I was naked and you clothed me, I was sick and you visited me, I was in prison and you came to me.' Then the righteous will answer him, 'Lord, when did we see thee hungry and feed thee, or thirsty and give thee drink? And when did we see thee a stranger and welcome thee, or naked and clothe thee? And when did we see thee sick or in prison and visit thee? And the King will answer them, 'Truly I say to you, as you did it to one of the least of these my brethren, you did it to me.' Then he will say to those at his left hand, 'Depart from me, you cursed, into the eternal fire prepared for the devil and his angels; for I was hungry and you gave me no food, I was thirsty and you gave me no drink, I was a stranger and you did not welcome me, naked and you did not clothe me, sick and in prison and you did not visit me.' Then they also will answer, 'Lord, when did we see thee hungry or thirsty or a stranger or naked or sick or in prison, and did not minister to thee?' Then he will answer them, 'Truly, I say to you, as you did it not to one of the least of these, you did it not to me.' And they will go away into eternal punishment, but the righteous into eternal life."

John 5 : 22-24   *The Father gives judgment to the Son*

The Father judges no one, but has given all judgment to the Son, that all may honour the Son, even as they honour the Father. He who does not honour the Son does not honour the Father who sent him. Truly, truly, I say to you, he who hears my word and believes him who sent me, has eternal life; he does not come into judgment, but has passed from death to life.

Reflection

Perfect love drives out fear, but there is an inescapable awesomeness about Christ; he cannot be entirely reduced to a gentle Jesus picture, affectionate to children and kindly to all. On earth he showed his power of command with an effectiveness that brooked no contradiction. Mark's gospel represents him as seeing the first four apostles beside the Lake and calling them, without any prelude, to follow him; such was his power of command that they followed him, and gladly. He commands the wind and the sea and they obey him; he commands diseases and evil spirits, and they are shattered at his word. And his judgment is fearless and uncompromising: he amazed the Pharisees and Scribes by the authority with which he taught: he sends a message to Herod

'Go, tell that fox. . ."' There is no 'please' or 'if you don't mind' or 'if you agree', but it is 'Sell all you have and follow me' without hesitation or yielding. Christ on earth was a figure of command. One could tell that in him God was judging.

Especially in John's gospel we see the theme of judgment during Christ's ministry and all his life. Men are judged, or judge themselves, by their reaction to Jesus; on this rock the great cleavage occurs, like a tide running towards a rock and dividing on either side of it. The judgment of God works itself out by whether men honour the Son and listen to his word or not; so that for one who does listen to his word there is no judgment, for he has already accepted life. The time of Christ's life on earth is truly a crisis, ending with the dreadful judgment scene before Pilate, where the Jewish authorities think they are securing the condemnation of Jesus, when they are in fact condemning themselves. When they cry 'We have no king but Caesar' Judaism falls to the ground: its authorities have denied the hope of God's saviour, the messianic king. On the rock which is Christ are they judged, and they founder.

But is this crisis period passed? It would be strange if one generation alone bore the crisis of the whole world. For each of us there is the same crisis through life, and Matthew's judgment scene shows how it occurs. In a way judgment has already occurred by the time of this scene, and Christ presides only over the sorting out. There is no calling of witnesses or establishment of evidence; it has all occurred in life, and each man recognizes the situation for what it is. It only needs the clarification that what was done to one of the least of his brethren was done to him. It is clear how our confrontation with Christ, and so our crisis, must occur. But loving our fellow men is not in itself enough: it must really be loving Christ in them.

Prayer

Let us not try to tame you, Lord, but in confidence also fear your judgment. We judge ourselves against you now; give us strength in this, our crisis.

22

THE EXEGESIS OF THE FATHER

John 1 : 1-5, 16-18   *The Word of the Father*

In the beginning was the Word, and the Word was with God, and the Word was God. He was in the beginning with God; all things were made through him, and without him was not anything made that was made. In him was life, and the life was the light of men. The light shines in the darkness, and the darkness has not overcome it.

. . . And from his fullness have we all received, grace upon grace. For the law was given through Moses; grace and truth came through Jesus Christ. No one has ever seen God; the only Son, who is in the bosom of the Father, he has made him known.

John 14 : 8-11a   *'Show us the Father'*

Philip said to him, "Lord, show us the Father, and we shall be satisfied." Jesus said to him, "Have I been with you so long, and yet you do not know me, Philip? He who has seen me has seen the Father; how can you say, 'Show us the Father'? Do you not believe that I am in the Father and the Father in me? The words that I say to you I do not speak on my own authority; but the Father who dwells in me does his works. Believe me that I am in the Father and the Father in me."

Reflection

In a way the clue to the incarnation is entirely contained in the last phrase of the prologue to St John's Gospel, 'the only Son who is in the bosom of the Father, has made him known'. The expression for 'made him known' is normally used of the explanation given by some interpreter of a difficult text, or by a lawyer of the implications of a law. The way it is used here is most unusual, as it is unusual for one person to explain or interpret another person. The incarnation is the interpretation into human terms of what God is. As Jesus' own saying in the later passage of John shows, the point of his becoming man was to show us the Father.

Anything we say of the Father must be accompanied by a host of contradictions, so that in the Eastern Church theologians have said that one can only say what God is not. Just as God's knowledge of all things is not only incomparably wider than any human knowledge but also of a totally different and higher quality than man's knowledge, so all his other qualities. A pet bird or fish can be taught to come to the hand that feeds it, and one might call this love. This is grotesque when such a relationship is compared to the subtlety, delicacy and warmth of the human relationship of love between two people. But in comparison to God's love, human love in all its beauty is far less rich than is the 'love' of a pet bird or fish in comparison to human love. This is why St Paul can say that all fatherhood in heaven and on earth takes its name from God the Father: human fatherhood, with its love, protective guidance, anxious but unfussing care — whatever qualities one considers necessary to ideal fatherhood — is a pale shadow of God's fatherhood.

So human nature can never contain any of the qualities of God, and we can never on earth fully understand them; we can do little more than stammer about them, for to be filled with an understanding of God is the happiness and wonder of heaven, and our task here below is to enlarge ourselves to reach the full depths of which we are capable, so as to receive as rich a relationship to God as possible. But Jesus is the translation into human terms, in the minimal measure that this is possible, of God, so that we may see a little in our terms what God means, and understand a little more of him.

The evangelist, with his deep and loving knowledge of Christ, picks out two qualities of God that 'came through Jesus Christ', his grace and his truth. His truth is really his fidelity, the fidelity of God to his people through thick and thin, through rebellion and ingratitude down the ages, the absolute trustworthiness and relia- bility of God which will never leave us in the lurch. His grace is the undeserved and boundless generosity of God, lavishing upon us with open hands, arms and heart all that we can take.

Prayer

Father in heaven, we can never reach more than a glimpse of your splendour, your might, or your love for us. Let me learn a little of you through your Son who brought you to us.

23

THE GLORY OF THE FATHER

John 2: 1-11   *The Son reveals his glory*

On the third day there was a marriage at Cana in
Galilee, and the mother of Jesus was there; Jesus also
was invited to the marriage, with his disciples. When the
wine failed, the mother of Jesus said to him, "They
have no wine." And Jesus said to her, "O woman, what
have you to do with me? My hour has not yet come."
His mother said to the servants, "Do whatever he tells
you." Now six stone jars were standing there, for the
Jewish rites of purification, each holding twenty or
thirty gallons. Jesus said to them, "Fill the jars with
water." And they filled them up to the brim. He said
to them, "Now draw some out, and take it to the
steward of the feast." So they took it. When the steward
of the feast tasted the water now become wine, and did
not know where it came from (though the servants who
had drawn the water knew), the steward of the feast
called the bridegroom and said to him, "Every man
serves the good wine first; and when men have drunk
freely, then the poor wine; but you have kept the good
wine until now." This, the first of his signs, Jesus did
at Cana in Galilee, and manifested his glory; and his
disciples believed in him.

"Father, I desire that they also, whom thou hast given me, may be with me where I am, to behold my glory which thou hast given me in thy love for me before the foundation of the world. O righteous Father, the world has not known thee, but I have known thee; and these know that thou hast sent me. I made known to them thy name, and I will make it known, that the love with which thou hast loved me may be in them, and I in them."

When Jesus had spoken these words, he went forth with his disciples across the Kidron valley, where there was a garden, which he and his disciples entered.

Reflection

From the beginning of his ministry Jesus speaks of his 'hour' with expectation. At Cana he says that his hour is not yet come; at various points in the story they do not arrest him because his hour has not yet come. When the end is approaching he says that the hour has come for the Son of Man to be glorified. And finally he prays 'Father, the hour has come; glorify thy Son that the Son may glorify thee'. The hour to which everything has been building up is, then, the glorification at the passion, death and resurrection, and the revelation of the glory of the Father and of the Son.

But in the words which immediately precede the passion, when Jesus is about to go out into the garden, what is being revealed is the mutual love of Father and Son, and their oneness. Two things are remarkable here. Firstly that Jesus regards this particular truth to be the summit of revelation: it is not the debasement of mankind or the evil of sin which is about to be revealed, nor the endurance required to win God's favour, nor the justice of God, nor even the love of Christ for mankind. It is precisely the love of the two persons for each other, a strictly intra-Trinitarian matter. Or is it so strictly intra-Trinitarian? Surely it must be that the love of Father and Son is so great that it overflows and diffuses itself to mankind, until mankind is bathed in the warmth of a love which is strictly the love of one divine Person for another; we are swept up by the same intensity of divine love. Another dimension is that Jesus who is a man is joined in such complete unity to the Father, and we are thereby, by our solidarity with him, also raised into the divine intimacy. This is what is intended as being the summit of revelation.

The other remarkable thing is that Jesus regards this love as being revealed precisely by his 'hour'. So often the passion is thought of as being the moment when Jesus pays the debt of us all, the debt of suffering. He suffers for us and satisfies the requirements of divine justice. Far from being a proof of unity of Father and Son, sometimes it is considered the moment when he feels himself abandoned by the Father and suffers the pains of the demand. In view of his final statement before the passion this will not do. Paul, in Romans, tells us that in the passion Christ fulfills the obedience which Adam denied. Now perfect obedience is a manifestation of love, and so when Christ is showing perfect obedience it must be not in a spirit of fear of the Father or abandonment by him, but in the fullest possible moment of love for him and union to him. This is why the passion is the climax of human life on earth, because at this moment humanity reaches its highest point of love for God, in the perfect re-uniting of man with God by Christ's loving obedience. This is why it is the hour of his glorification, issuing in the manifestation of this at the resurrection.

Prayer

Lord Jesus, it was my sin which brought about this fullest revelation of your love for the Father, and so of my sharing in that love. Raise me with you by the perfect love of obedience to your will and his to the Father's side. Make me realize that, as in your case, any suffering I am sent is a proof of your love and a challenge of mine.

24

CHRIST OUR LORD

1 Corinthians 8 : 5-6 *One God and one Lord*

For although there may be so-called gods in heaven or on earth — as indeed there are many "gods" and many "lords" — yet for us there is one God, the Father, from whom are all things and for whom we exist, and one Lord, Jesus Christ, through whom are all things and through whom we exist.

1 Corinthians 12 : 3 *Confession of Jesus as Lord*

Therefore I want you to understand that no one speaking by the Spirit of God ever says "Jesus be cursed!" and no one can say "Jesus is Lord" except by the Holy Spirit.

Reflection

These two little passages show between them how the whole Trinity stands to us, or other how we stand to the Trinity. But first one asks what the difference is between 'God' and 'Lord'. The terms are often synonymous in Jewish Greek, for 'Lord' is used to translate 'Yahweh', the Hebrew personal name of God; so when

Jesus is called Lord there is no hint that he is inferior to God or to the Father. If there is any difference between the two terms it is perhaps that the Lord is more immediate. One is more conscious of his power and dominion, which enters more into the weave of everyday life. The title Lord was, after all, used very commonly of any powerful figure, and could be used simply as a respectful address, like 'Sir', so it would be a more familiar term of common life, and suggest someone whose influence and domination are not remote but very present realities.

In the case of Jesus Christ in our first passage, his present force as Lord is especially felt. Firstly, he spans the present period of history as Lord, for he became Lord by the resurrection, and his Lordship will be completed when he returns as Lord — the two poles of this present last period in history. Secondly, it is suggested by the very terms Paul uses: there is a double movement in progress, from and to the Father, and each of these is through Christ. All things are *from* the Father and we exist *for* him; thus he is the ultimate both as origin and as term. He is the Alpha and the Omega, the beginning and the end of all things, who therefore in every sense gives all things their purpose. Parallel to this are clearly the two statements about Christ. He is the agent of creation, the wisdom of God through whom he creates the world. It is hard to understand this position, a person who is the medium of creation. We can understand that a person can be an agent of creation, and we can understand that God can create through and in and by his wisdom, using his wisdom as the medium of creation, the model by which he works. Yet it is only if we can fathom how the person of Christ is the wisdom on the model of which God created the world that we can appreciate how basically we were created through Christ. By parallel, when it is said that we exist through Christ, it should be that through Christ we exist for God, that our way to God is through Christ, he is the model and the medium by which we go to God. So central is he to our whole existence.

And yet it is only through faith that we can recognise this and reach the sense of our existence. Only through the Spirit of God can we call Jesus 'Lord' and by so doing recognize his centrality and dominance of our lives. Thus the circle is completed and the whole Trinity plays a part in our lives if they are to be objective and reach their goal.

Prayer

Lord God, Jesus was exalted at the resurrection to become Lord at your right hand, and it is through him that we exist and come to you. We thank you for this dignity conferred on human nature and for the hope it gives us too. Help us to submit ourselves totally to him, to be created by him and recreated in his image.

25

MARANATHA

1 Thessalonians 5:1-10   *The Lord comes like a thief in the night*

But as to the times and the seasons, brethren, you have no need to have anything written to you. For you yourselves know well that the day of the Lord will come like a thief in the night. When people say, "There is peace and security," then sudden destruction will come upon them as travail comes upon a woman with child, and there will be no escape. But you are not in darkness, brethren, for that day to surprise you like a thief. For you are all sons of light and sons of the day; we are not of the night or of darkness. So then let us not sleep, as others do, but let us keep awake and be sober. For those who sleep sleep at night, and those who get drunk are drunk at night. But, since we belong to the day, let us be sober, and put on the breastplate of faith and love, and for a helmet the hope of salvation. For God has not destined us for wrath, but to obtain salvation through our Lord Jesus Christ, who died for us so that whether we wake or sleep we might live with him.

1 Corinthians 16:21-24   *Maranatha*

I, Paul, write this greeting with my own hand. If any one has no love for the Lord, let him be accursed.

Maranatha! The grace of the Lord Jesus be with you. My love be with you all in Christ Jesus. Amen.

1 Corinthians 15:24-28   *The consummation*

Then comes the end, when he delivers the kingdom to God the Father after destroying every rule and every authority and power. For he must reign until he has put all his enemies under his feet. The last enemy to be destroyed is death. "For God has put all things in subjection under his feet." But when it says, "All things are put in subjection under him," it is plain that he is excepted who put all things under him. When all things are subjected to him, then the Son himself will also be subjected to him who put all things under him, that God may be everything to every one.

Reflection

The day of the Lord mentioned in the first passage is the traditional expression in the Bible for the final cataclysm, when the Jews expected God to come and put an end to the world as we know it, judging the wicked and rewarding the just. In the New Testament it is the Lord Jesus who has taken on this role, as so many other divine roles and properties are transferred to him; he will come to do the work of God at the last day. The part which this day of the Lord played in the Christian imagination is shown by *Maranatha* in the second passage: it is an Aramaic expression retained even in Paul's Greek, a sure sign that it is a specially loved expression, so full of meaning for the early Christians that they kept it in the original language even though Greek was their language. It means 'Our Lord, come!' or perhaps 'The Lord is coming'. Its retention in the original shows how vivid and important was the Christians' hope for the coming of the Lord.

We no longer expect any immediate coming of the Lord with cosmic disaster and a judgment of the whole human race. Nevertheless some echo of this persists in the Christian imagination, and certainly the backcloth of the Christian hope is that in the end the Lord will set to rights all injustices, reward those who have been persecuted or have suffered for his sake and give to those who have turned away from him the only reward which they are capable of receiving. We do not need so much the scenario of stars falling from heaven and earthquakes; more satisfying is the passage from First Corinthians which describes the consummation of the kingdom. At this time Christ's lordship will be completed, that lordship over creation into which entered the humanity of Christ at his own resurrection and exaltation, will achieve its final stage when he delivers the kingdom to his Father.

It is paradoxical that the moment at which the Son's kingdom reaches its fullness is the moment at which he hands it back to his Father. But here again the perfect obedience of the Son is at work, that same perfect obedience which reconciled the world to God in the crucifixion. Now it is like a triple split image coming into focus: the consummation of the world is that it should be perfectly subjected to the Son, and his own consummation is that he should submit all things to the Father; thus the two lower images come into the focus of perfect obedience to the Father. On our own personal scale the same is true: the more we abandon ourselves to God in whose image we are made, and to Christ in whom we are re-created, the more we find ourselves and reach our full perfection. By obedience to God we become more, not less, free; by being filled with Christ we become more, not less, ourselves. And by so doing we hasten the consummation of the world in Christ, the perfection which was the purpose of the incarnation.

Prayer

Lord God, you sent your Son into the world that he might take it to himself and submit it all to you. Grant that I may submit myself more perfectly to him and by taking on his image achieve your will in me.